CAMBRIDGE UNIVERSITY PRESS

CAMBRIDGE ENGLISH
Language Assessment
Part of the University of Cambridge

CAMBRIDGE OFFICIAL PREPARATION MATERIAL

Updated Second Edition

T0372597

Starter Class Book
with CD-ROM
American English

Caroline Nixon & Michael Tomlinson

Language summary

Key vocabulary

Key grammar and functions

1 Hi!
page 4

Character names:
Marie, Maskman, Monty

Numbers:
one, two, three, four, five, six

What's your name?
I'm ...
How old are you?
I'm ...

2 My class
page 10

Classroom objects:
bag, book, chair, eraser, pencil, table

Imperatives:
open your books, close your books, stand up, sit down, listen, look, point

What's this?
It's a ...

Marie's math Shapes
page 16

circle, triangle, square

Trevor's values Ask nicely
page 17

Pass me the ... please.
Here you are.
Thank you.

3 My colors
page 18

Colors:
black, blue, brown, red, white, yellow

Adjectives:
It's red.
It's a red pencil.

What's your favorite color?
It's ...

4 My toys
page 24

Toys:
ball, bike, car, doll, kite, robot

Where's ... ?
It's here.
... isn't here.

Marie's art Butterfly colors
page 30

orange, green, pink

Trevor's values Giving
page 31

Mommy, Daddy
Here's a ... for you.

Review  page 32

1 Hi!

1 CD1 2 Listen and point.

2 CD1 3 Say the chant.

4

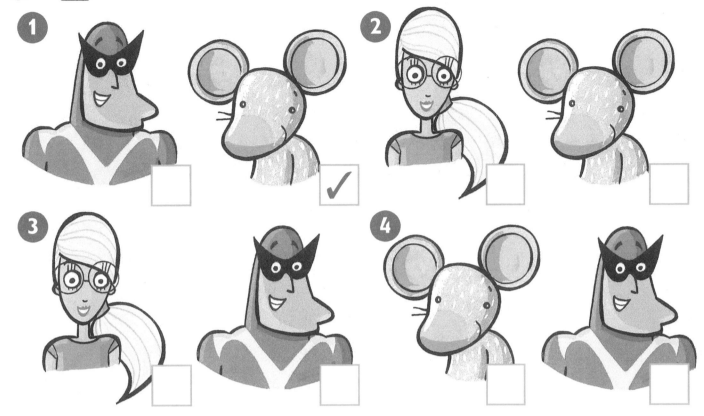

3 🔊 ✏️ Listen and check (✓).

1

□   ✓

2

□   □

3

□   □

4

□   □

4 🔍 ✏️ Look and draw. Say the number.

1

3	1	2
3	3	1
2	1	3

2

1	3	2
3	2	2
3	1	2

3

2	3	1
3	1	2
1	1	3

4

2	1	1
1	3	2
3	3	3

Marie   Maskman   Monty   one   two   three   What's your name?   I'm ...

6  Look and draw. Say the numbers.

2	••
6	
3	

5	
1	
4	

7 Listen and circle.

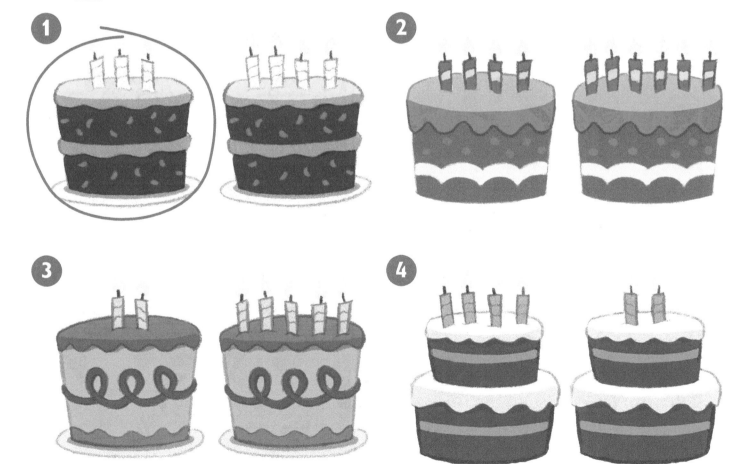

1

2

3

4

four   five   six   How old are you?   I'm ...   **7**

8  Listen to the story.

9  Listen and stick.

10 Talk to Maskman.

2 My class

1 🔊 11 CD1 🦋 Listen and point.

2 🔊 12 CD1 💬 Say the chant.

3 🔊 13 CD1 ✏️ Listen and circle the number.

1 4 ⑤

2 2 3

3 3 4

4 2 3

5 5 6

6 1 2

4 🔍 ✏️ Look and complete.

1 ?

2 ?

3 ?

bag book chair eraser pencil table

Listen and point. Sing the song.

6 🔊 **16** CD1 ✏️ Listen and check (✓).

7 ✏️💬 Draw your classroom. Say.

Me!

Listen to the story.

9 🔊 **CD1 18** 👦 Listen and stick.

10 🔊 **CD1 19** 💬 Talk to Maskman.

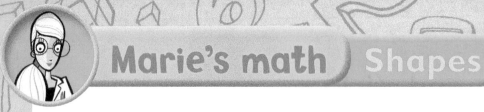
1  Listen and point. Say the chant.

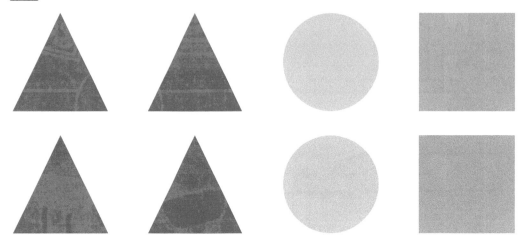

2 Look and count. Make and say.

circle   triangle   square

3 21 CD1 Listen and point.

4 Act it out.

3 My colors

2 23 CD1 Say the chant.

3

✏️ **Listen and draw lines.**

1 **2** **3**

4 ✏️ **Listen and color.**

1 **2** **3** **4** **5** **6**

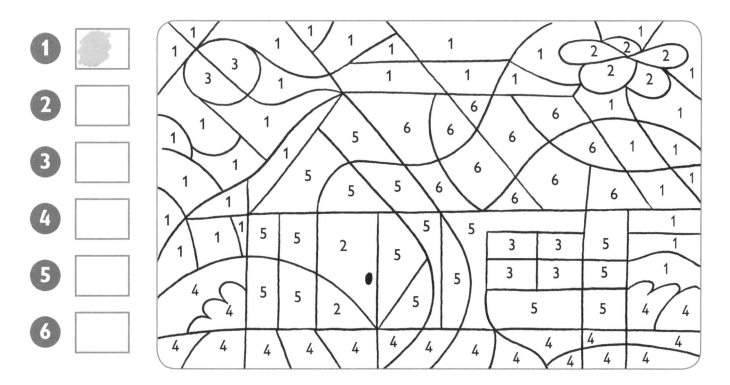

black   blue   brown   red   white   yellow   **19**

20

6  CD1 28 ✏️ Listen and color.

1 **2** **3**

4 **5** **6**

7 CD1 29 💬 Listen, count, and answer.

It's red.   It's a red pencil. **21**

9 CD1 31 Listen and stick.

10 CD1 32 Talk to Maskman.

4 My toys

1 Listen and point.

2 Say the chant.

24

3  **35** CD1 ✏️ Listen and color.

1

2

3

4

4 **36** CD1 ✏️ Listen and draw lines.

1 2 3 4

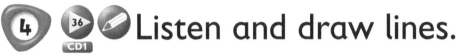

ball bike car doll kite robot **25**

6  **Listen and write the number.**

7 **Draw your favorite toy. Say.**

Me!

8 🎧 40 CD1 Listen to the story.

9 **41** CD1 **Listen and stick.**

10 **42** CD1 **Talk to Maskman.**

?

1 🔍✏️ **Look and draw lines.**

2 🧍💬 **Make a butterfly. Say the colors.**

3  Listen and point.

4  Act it out.

Mommy   Daddy   Here's a ... for you.   31

Review

1 🎧 44 CD1 ✏️ **Listen and circle the number.**

1  ⑤ 6

2  2 3

3  3 4

4  1 2

2 🎧 45 CD1 ✏️ **Listen, count, and color.**

1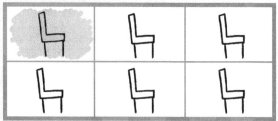

2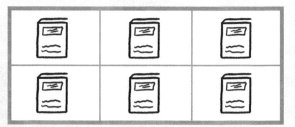

3

4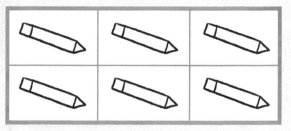

5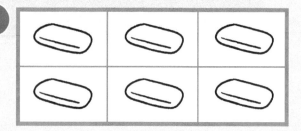

6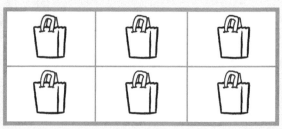

3 🔊46 CD1 ✏️ Listen and color.

1 **2** **3** **4** **5** **6**

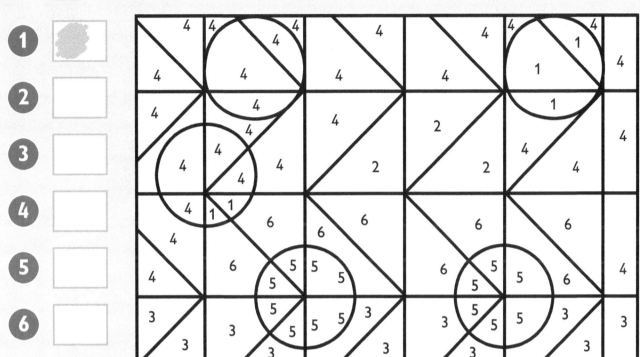

4 🔊47 CD1 ✏️ Listen and write the number.

1

5 My house

1 **CD2** Listen and point.

2 **CD2** Say the chant.

34

3 CD2 **4** ✏️ Listen and circle.

4 CD2 **5** ✏️ Listen and color.

6 ▶8 CD2 ✎ Listen and draw lines.

1

2

3

4

7 ▶9 CD2 ✎ Listen and follow.

in   on   under   He's ...   She's ...   **37**

8 **CD2 10** Listen to the story.

9 **11** CD2 Listen and stick.

10 **12** CD2 Talk to Maskman.

6 My body

1 CD2 13 Listen and point.

2 CD2 14 Say the chant.

40

3  **Listen and write the number.**

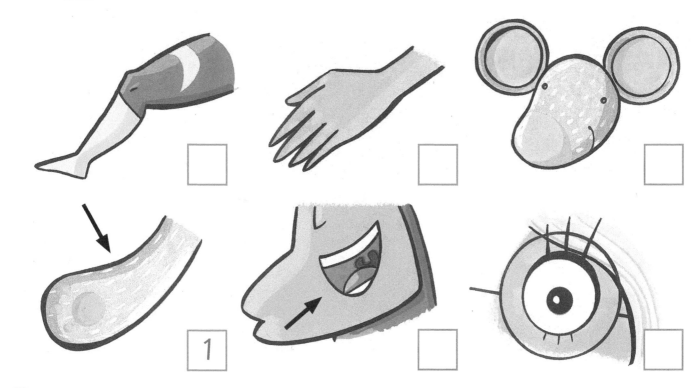

4 Look and complete.

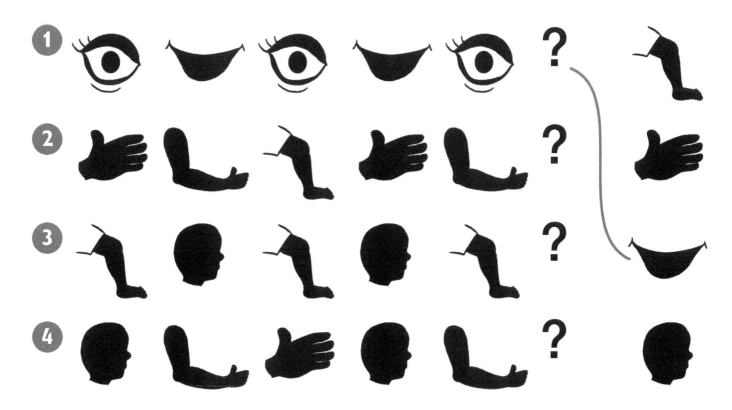

arm   eye   hand   head   leg   mouth

5 16 CD2 Listen and point. Sing the song.

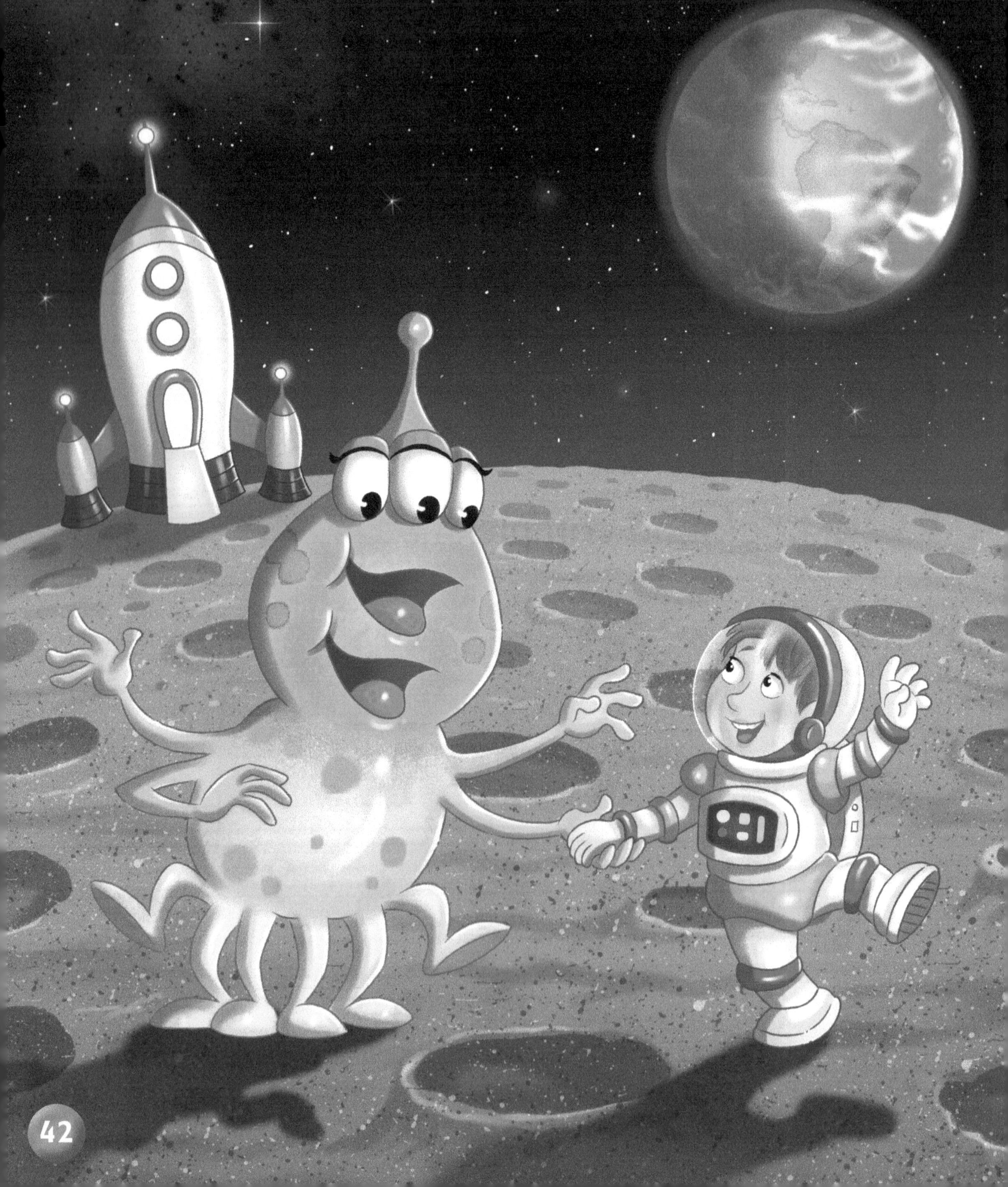

6 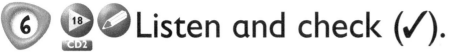 Listen and check (✓).

1 ☐ ✓

2 ☐ ☐

3 ☐ ☐

4 ☐ ☐

5 ☐ ☐

6 ☐ ☐

7 Draw an alien. Say.

Me!

8 **19** **CD2** Listen to the story.

44

9 **20** CD2 Listen and stick.

10 **21** CD2 Talk to Maskman.

?

1 22 CD2 ✏ Listen and write the number.

2 Make a book. Say.

3 Listen and point.

4 Act it out.

Let's play Pairs. OK. You start. It's my turn.

7 My animals

1 **24** CD2 Listen and point.

2 **25** CD2 Say the chant.

3  Listen and follow.

4 Listen and draw lines.

6 🎵 **30** CD2 ✏️ Listen and check (✓).

1
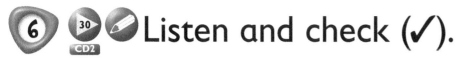

2

3

4

7 🎵 **31** CD2 ✏️ Listen and write the number.

I can ... I can't ... fly jump swim **51**

32 CD2 Listen to the story.

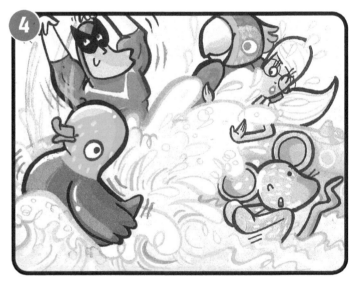

9 **33** CD2 **Listen and stick.**

1 2 3 4 5 6

10 **34** CD2 **Talk to Maskman.**

?

8 My food

1  Listen and point.

2 Say the chant.

3 🎧37 CD2 ✏️ Listen and circle.

1 **2** **3**

4 **5** **6**

4 🔍 ✏️ Look and complete.

1 ?

2 ?

3 ?

4 ?

cake   egg   fries   fruit   milk   tomato   **55**

6  Listen and write the number.

7 Draw foods you like and don't like. Say.

8  Listen to the story.

9 **42** CD2  Listen and stick.

1

2

3

4

5

6

10 **43** CD2 Talk to Maskman.

?

1 44 CD2 ✏️ Listen and write the number.

2 👤💬 Make a poster. Say.

3   Listen and point.

4 Act it out.

Review

1 🔊46 CD2 ✏️ Listen and draw lines.

2 🔊47 CD2 ✏️ Listen and circle.

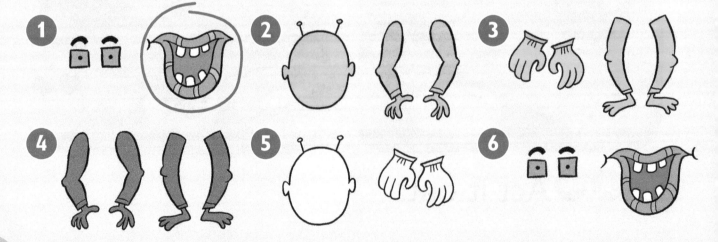

3 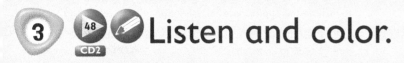 Listen and color.

4 Listen and draw lines.

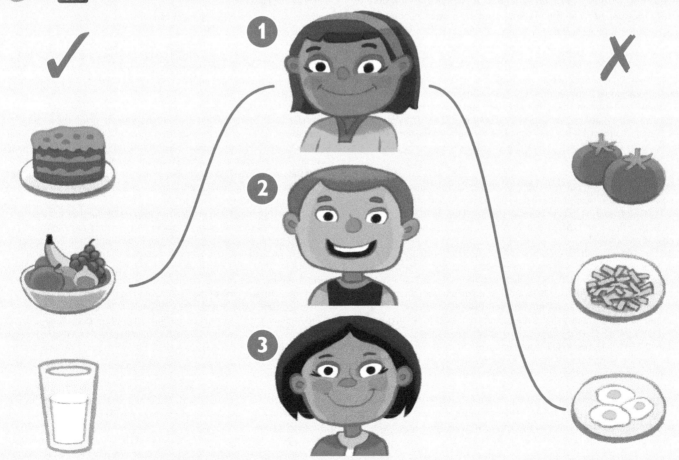

Thanks and Acknowledgments

Authors' thanks

Many thanks to everyone at Cambridge University Press and in particular to:

Rosemary Bradley for supervising the whole project and using her fine organizational skills to bring it all together;

Colin Sage for all his hard work, enthusiasm, keen eye for detail, and invaluable input;

Emily Hird for getting the ball rolling and overseeing the development of the project;

Susan Norris-Roberts for coming back on board with her professional experience, expertise, and invaluable advice.

Dedications

To Lydia and Silvia, with all my love. CN

To Paloma. Thank you for all your love, help, and support along the way. MT

The Authors and Publishers would like to thank the following teachers for their help in reviewing the material and for the invaluable feedback they provided:

Russia: Irina Polyakova, Lyceum Stolichny; Zahra Bilides, Language Link. Turkey: Ebru Vural and Nural Edizsoy, Maya Koleji; Maria Topkar, Çevre Private School.

We would also like to thank all the teachers who allowed us to observe their classes and who gave up their invaluable time for interviews and focus groups.

The authors and publishers acknowledge the following sources of copyright material and are grateful for the permissions granted. While every effort has been made, it has not always been possible to identify the sources of all the material used or to trace all copyright holders. If any omissions are brought to our notice, we will be happy to include the appropriate acknowledgments on reprinting.

p. 17 (background): Thinkstock; p. 30 (pink & blue butterfly): Shutterstock/suns07; p. 30 (orange butterfly): Shutterstock/Sari ONeal; p. 30 (green & red butterfly): Shutterstock/Aleksandr Kurganov; p. 31 (background): Thinkstock; p. 46 (tree): Shutterstock/Le Do; p. 46 (logs): Shutterstock/koya979; p. 46 (table): Shutterstock/Chukcha; p. 46 (door): Shutterstock/YK; p. 46 (house): Shutterstock/bioraven; p.46 (bed): Shutterstock/sagir; p. 46 (chair): Shutterstock/Chamille White; p. 17 (background): Thinkstock; p. 60 (frog spawn): Shutterstock/DJTaylor; p. 60 (tadpole): DP Wildlife Vertebrates/Alamy; p. 60 (frog): Shutterstock/Matthijs Wetterauw; p. 61 (background): Thinkstock.

Commissioned photography on pages 16, 30B, 46B, 60B by Trevor Clifford Photography.

The authors and publishers are grateful to the following illustrators:

Beatrice Costamagna, c/o Pickled ink; Chris Jones; Helen Naylor, c/o Plum Pudding; Kelly Kennedy, c/o Sylvie Poggio; Melanie Sharp, c/o Sylvie Poggio; Richard Hoit, Beehive; Xian Xio, c/o Illustrationweb

The publishers are grateful to the following contributors:

Louise Edgeworth: picture research and art direction
Wild Apple Design Ltd: page design
Blooberry: additional design
Lon Chan: cover design
Melanie Sharp: cover illustration
John Green and Tim Woolf, TEFL Audio: audio recordings
John Marshall Media, Inc. and Lisa Hutchins: audio recordings for the American English edition
Robert Lee: song writing
hyphen S.A.: publishing managment, American English edition

Hi! (page 9)

 My class (page 15)

 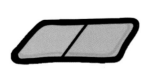 

3 **My colors** (page 23)

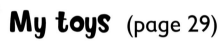 **4** **My toys** (page 29)

 **Unit stars**

5 **My house** (page 39)

6 **My body** (page 45)

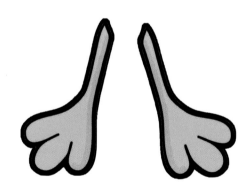

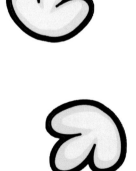

7 # My animals (page 53)

 **8** # My food (page 59)

Unit stars